USHERING 101

Easy Steps to Ushering in the Local Church

by
Buddy Bell

Harrison House
Tulsa, Oklahoma

Ushering 101:
Easy Steps to Ushering in the Local Church
ISBN 1-57794-163-2
Copyright © 1996 by Buddy Bell
P.O. Box 27366
Tulsa, Oklahoma 74149

05 04 03 02   8 7 6 5 4

Published by Harrison House, Inc.
P.O. Box 35035
Tulsa, Oklahoma 74153

Contents

Foreword

Buddy Bell, a leader in training effective, Spirit-led ushers, pours his years of knowledge and experience into this book. He trains ushers to be prepared and organized and aware that their ministry is one of the most important in the church. Through practical teaching, creatively and humorously presented, Buddy Bell covers every aspect of ushering including concerns of the nineties.

The usher who reads this book and learns how to confidently handle every situation he might encounter will be free to represent Jesus and the heart of the church as he fulfills his calling in the ministry of helps. When the ministry of helps operates in the love and wisdom of God, visitors come back, needs of the people are met and potential disturbances are handled before they occur. I highly recommend this book to every current or potential usher committed to serving his local church and God in excellence.

—John C. Maxwell, D. Min.
Founder, Injoy, Inc.
Leadership Development Training

Acknowledgments

I wish to thank my wife, Kathy, and my daughters Jennifer, Brandee, Stephanie and Kendra for their patience and understanding through the years when many times they were without a husband and a daddy. They believed in the calling and the anointing that was upon me and this ministry. Behind every man of God, there is a great woman of God.

I also want to thank Marcus and Regina Mays for their devoted friendship and help in writing this book for ushers.

Finally, many thanks to Christopher Parks, a very gifted and talented Christian lawyer, for his contributions to this book. And, let's not forget Noah!

Introduction

Welcome potential usher! You are about to embark on one of the greatest and most challenging areas of ministry in the Church today. Your responsibilities can be summed up in five words— leaders, greeters, meeters, seaters and helpers. There is never a dull moment when you commit to this area of the helps ministry.

You will not only assist the pastor in accomplishing the goals for the congregation, but you will function in a crucial public relations role for the church. Your love for serving others and commitment to excellence in this area will manifest much fruit in the lives of others.

This book covers both the biblical and practical aspects of church ushering. This book is designed to bring organization and efficiency to the local church while developing a committed and godly ushering staff. Understanding the scriptural role of ushering, I believe, will revolutionize your heart and mind as a current or potential usher.

For too long, the Church has ignored the ministry of helps as described in the Apostle Paul's first letter to the Corinthian church:

> **And God hath set some in the church, first apostles, secondarily prophets, thirdly teachers, after that miracles, then gifts of**

healing, HELPS, **governments, diversities of tongues.**

1 Corinthians 12:28

I believe as you realize the importance of this God—ordained and God—anointed ministry of helps, you will see your local church blossom with the excellence the Lord intended. My intention is to motivate church members to support and assist the pastor in fulfilling the divine calling for your congregation.

I encourage you as you serve in the area of ushering to constantly communicate with the pastor to understand the vision for the Church and ministry. This will motivate you to continually improve your level of dedication and service. Positions such as ushering should be a privilege and not a "have-to." Your motivation is simply to be a success by fulfilling everything God has for you. If you have a positive goal to attain, you will see greater and greater results.

I encourage you to be honest with yourself. You must truly believe God wants you to minister in the area of ushering in order to be truly effective. Don't accept the responsibility because it just seems like "the thing to do" or because your best friends are doing it.

If you don't believe you are called to be an usher, don't allow yourself to feel pressured to participate. You must believe that the Lord raises up the individuals He intends for this ministry. However, don't be discouraged because you feel inexperienced or lack the ability to quiet screaming babies. The best ministers of helps are people like you with a servant's heart. If you serve with a humble heart, God will abundantly bless you with ability for the job and surround you with His favor.

Never get so involved in small details that you forget that you are doing more than straightening chairs, seating people and passing offering buckets. You are an anointed, supernaturally equipped door-keeper in the house of God.

—Rev. Buddy Bell
Ministry of Helps International

PART 1

Ushers—
Your Church's
Most Valuable Asset

1
The Role of Ushering in the Local Church

The Scriptural Foundation for Ushering

Ushering in your local church involves much more than shaking hands and shining your shoes. Some churches think that ushers are just bucket passers, so they grab anybody to pass the bucket. "Let's just grab ol' Larry when he comes walking in. Let's just get anybody." You don't want to get just *anybody*, because you don't want an *anybody* offering. You have been selected as an usher; you are in the ministry of helps, employed by Almighty God.

> **And God hath set some in the church, first apostles, secondarily prophets, thirdly teachers, after that miracles, then gifts of healing, HELPS, governments, diversities of tongues.**
>
> **1 Corinthians 12:28**

Many people have never noticed the ministry of helps in the Bible. They have noticed apostles, prophets, teachers, miracles, gifts of healings, tongues and interpretation. But when it comes to helps and governments, many people say, "I must have blinked and missed that one." They blinked because "helps" didn't sound very important.

But God has set the ministry of helps into the Church. You as an usher in your church, fall within the ministry of helps category.

This Scripture reveals several important truths:

1. Your ministry is ordained and anointed by God Himself. You have been divinely set in the Church for a purpose.

2. Your ministry in helps is just as important as other leadership

offices such as the apostle and prophet.

3. It is a supernatural ministry like miracles and healing.

The word helps comes from the Greek word *antilepsis* or *antilempsis* which means "a laying hold of, an exchange...lay hold of, so as to support."[1] Its literal meaning is "one who gives assistance." *Helps* describes "one of the ministrations in the local church, by way of rendering assistance, perhaps especially of help ministered to the weak and needy."[2]

---

[1] W. E. Vine, *An Expository Dictionary of New Testament Words*, (Old Tappan, New Jersey: Fleming H. Revell, 1940), s.v. "HELP."

[2] Ibid.

In other words, if you are helping anyone in the church or assisting the weak and needy, you are operating in the ministry of helps.

Is Ushering Biblical?

Envisioning an usher usually conjures up an image of a white-shirted, gloved man wandering through a movie theater with a flashlight. Church people think of bucket-passers and hand-shakers, but the Bible reveals ushers to be trusted men who handle the many details of ruling and serving God's people. The Greek word *diakonos*[3] used

---

[3] James Strong, *Greek Dictionary of the New Testament*, in Strong's Exhaustive Concordance of the Bible, (Nashville: Abingdon, 1890) 76, #1249.

in First Timothy 3:8 and throughout the New Testament describes the first deacons in the church.

Their responsibilities included waiting on tables, feeding widows in the church and relieving the church leaders from the encumbering details of daily church operation. Today the office of deacon is most commonly filled by the usher.

Just like first century deacons, today's deacons rarely hold policy-making power. Their commission entails faithfully carrying out the desires and instructions of the pastor through the power of the Holy Spirit.

Remember the biblical account in Acts regarding the disciples' search for men to serve tables:

> **Wherefore, brethren, look ye out among you seven men of honest report, full of the Holy Ghost and wisdom, whom we may appoint over this business. But we will give ourselves continually to prayer, and to the ministry of the word. And the saying pleased the whole multitude: and they chose Stephen, a man full of faith and of the Holy Ghost.**
>
> **Acts 6:3-5**

This passage in Acts 6 sets the divine pattern for ushering in the Church. If Stephen was known and chosen because

he *was full of faith and the Holy Ghost,*
how much more should you strive for
this status and reputation?

But Stephen didn't stop there:

> **And Stephen, full of faith and**
> **power, did great wonders and**
> **miracles among the people.**
>
> **Acts 6:8**

In Acts 7, he boldly preached the
Gospel to the Sanhedrin, the supreme
council of the Jewish people, that
condemned Jesus and imprisoned Peter
and the other apostles in Acts 5:17-40.

Tasks Involved in Ushering

Many churches seem to demoralize
an usher's duties, thinking they are very

limited and unimportant. However, the duties of an usher range far beyond passing buckets and shaking hands and encompass weighty and meaningful tasks. I specifically define these duties in four areas.

Assist the Pastor

First of all, an usher assists the pastor and helps him bring his vision for the local church to fulfillment. As an usher, your presence will build up and add to the well-being of your church. The pastor stands up and says, "It's time for an offering." When an army of ushers stand and come forth, that impresses people. They think, "Wow, look at those people who are here to serve." Sadly, in some churches, when the pastor gets up to take an offering, he has to say, "Could we have some help? Is there anybody here who wants to serve God? Somebody jump up, and give us a hand here! We need some help over here or over there." People are watching this thinking "Hmm, I wonder what's going on around here? Nobody wants to assist the pastor."

Meet and Greet

Secondly, an usher is God's public relations man and represents the church to every new visitor. Because the pastor of a large church cannot personally greet all the people before a service, it is the usher's responsibility to make visitors feel welcome and important.

Now, I will discuss this in more detail a little later, but keep something in mind. Sometimes if an usher greets someone and the person falls down, the usher thinks it's the anointing of God that knocks them down. But it isn't the anointing; it's his breath. We call it dragon's breath. No matter how friendly the usher's "we just want to welcome you" is, his dragon's breath will knock them down and they will remember that!

I am covering some really personal things, but ushering is all about dealing with people. You would be amazed at the excuses people use for not coming to church. The next Sunday morning when they wake up, do you know who they think of first? Ol' dragon breath. And they pray that ol' dragon breath isn't at that door when they come in, because they already have their hair permed, and don't need another one!

Ushers should greet visitors with the same warmth and love as the pastor would himself. The usher has the unique privilege to make the first, and usually lasting, impression on a person. He can ease the visitor's transition from uneasy curiosity to security and enjoyment.

I have seen visitors track down a friendly usher before they leave the service and say, "We'll be back. You can count on us!" Why? They know they have a friend with a warm smile waiting when they return. You can make a difference in someone's life.

If you flow in your role, you will become the world's greatest salesman because you have what the public wants. In other words, you will be right there to help them with what they need. Your love and efficiency will impact visitors because you have:

- Warmly welcomed them with an outstretched hand and smile.

- Seated them in comfortable, accessible seats.

- Provided them with bulletins, songsheets and all necessary information on your church.

- Even gone the extra mile and told them you enjoyed their presence in the service and how much you would like them to come to a service again.

Maintain Order

The third task of the usher is to maintain order and orchestrate movement during the service and prayer ministry lines. First Corinthians 14:40 clearly reads, **Let all things be done decently and in order.** To achieve this harmony, you must know your spiritual authority and be a "watchman on the wall." After all, you are one of God's main safeguards against Satan's devices of confusion and distraction.

Consider yourself a guardian of God's anointed—the one who prevents needless human interruptions in the form of talkers and rovers. You are the first line of defense against the diversions that can separate people from God's Word and the flow of the Holy Spirit.

Note the exhortations issued in First Thessalonians 5:14,15. They provide an excellent basis for maintaining order.

- WARN them that are unruly,

- COMFORT the feeble-minded,

- SUPPORT the weak,

- BE PATIENT toward all men.

Maintaining order also involves being alert for any suspicious movement toward the stage. Don't allow anyone to make an unauthorized movement toward the pastor's platform.

If they do, escort them out quickly and quietly.

Be especially alert during:

- Times of crisis

- Spiritual conflict in your community

- Special meetings with well-known ministers

A pastor's stand for community righteousness, or a guest speaker's reputation for supernatural ministry can generate potentially violent actions.

We don't like to think about these things, but they have happened— violent things have gone on in churches. I was attacked at one time, in a service. Can you believe that? And I'm such a lovable guy! That experience inspired a new message I give called, "Where were the ushers when the preacher was being beat up?"

About twenty minutes into my message, I was emphasizing, "Ohhhh, the infinite value of the humble gospel helpers," when I heard someone say something on the other side of the sanctuary.

I'm the type of person that if you respond to me, I respond back to you. So I walked over, and there was a gentleman sitting on the second row who was saying something. He had even leaned over and said something to the person beside him. I said, "What's the problem?" He said, "You're too loud!" And I said,

"Brother, I've got to be loud. There are some people in here with thick heads."

Now, I have to admit, maybe I shouldn't have said that! But this guy just erupted. And I mean *violently*.

He started throwing people around! I leaned out to the man causing the disturbance. I patted him on the shoulder, and said, "Brother, calm down." He reached up and "Waack!", slapped me across the face. And this is in the middle of Sunday morning service!

Then he grabbed my hand, shoved it into his mouth and started biting me! He was holding my hand in his mouth, and blood was running down my hand. I looked at that and I looked at him, and I thought, "I've got a devil here! Or the devil's got me!"

About this time, I thought, "*Where* are the ushers?" Everybody was backed up, with a look on their faces that said, "Let's give him room. Let's see what's going to happen here!"

And then something did happen. Up to this point, I was very concerned about the service and all the people there. But then I literally felt like a coat was being taken off of me and another coat was put on me. The moment this coat or cloak touched me, I knew what it was. It was the anointing for the ministry of helps. My first thought was, "Neither give place to the devil." (Eph. 4:27).

One of our responsibilities as an usher is to make sure there are no disturbances in our services. We're here to cover all the bases.

And so when that cloak, that anointing touched me, I knew what I was supposed to do—get that person out of the service. I literally ripped my hand out of his mouth, grabbed him and said, "Sir, come on, we need to get out of here."

Then the ushers showed up and helped me! We took this gentleman out of the service and tried to minister to him. We tried to explain to him that you just don't act like that, and tried to determine what the problem was. He just wouldn't receive anything. I thought, "I can't go back out into the sanctuary, I mean, this is really embarrassing, to get beat up on Sunday morning while I'm preaching, let alone, bitten." But I thought, "I can't hide from them."

So I went back out and preached one of the shortest sermons I've ever preached. I said, "People, I'm not going to ignore what happened this morning. You saw what the devil can do with a person. That was not God. You can see what happens when the devil grabs hold of your life. And this is my message today, 'Who has hold of your life?'

"Does God have hold of your life? Or does the devil have hold of your life? It's possible that if the devil has hold of your life, you might turn out like this and react this way someday." Seven people rededicated their lives back to the Lord that day. Two whole families came forward and rededicated their lives. God received the glory in spite of the devil's best efforts to disrupt. But the point is, had those ushers understood their authority, this situation could have been avoided.

Receive Offerings

The fourth task of the usher is to receive offerings in a cheerful manner. I believe your attitude will affect the congregation's willingness to give to the Lord. Offerings actually have increased in churches after ushers were taught how to receive them.

In other words, don't wear a look on your face that indicates bankruptcy.

When it's time for the offering, usually the minister will say, "Now God loves a cheerful giver. God loves a hilarious giver. Put a smile on your face! We have an opportunity to give!" In most churches, the minister who is taking the offering usually encourages the people to be cheerful.

Then the ushers come down the aisle looking like they are at a funeral. They look like they're probably going to take the offering out back and bury it somewhere.

One person told me, "Brother Bell, that is so true. Last Sunday I was sitting in one of our services getting ready to write out my offering check, and I looked at one of our ushers. I said to myself, 'Honey, if you don't want it, I've got bills to pay.'" That usher was telling people, "I don't want your offering."

I've seen ushers tell congregations, "I don't think it's time for the offering," and not say anything with their mouthes. Eighty-five percent of communication is done through body expression.

How many times has someone walked up to you and said, "Hey, what's wrong?" And you said, "Well, nothing's wrong." They said, "You need to tell your face, because your face is telling everybody there's something wrong."

It takes thirty-five fewer muscles to smile than it does to frown. Some people wonder why they are worn out at the end of the day. I tell them, "You've been frowning all day. I'll make your day easier. I'll make it so you'll use thirty-five fewer muscles during the day—just practice smiling."

In other words, don't wear a look on your face that indicates bankruptcy! If the pastor announces a second unexpected offering, don't groan or let your face express disappointment at the break in your routine. You are a leader in the Church, so be cautious that you do not reflect wrong attitudes to others.

When you serve people, you must leave your burdens at Jesus' feet and let His love radiate from your face. Victorious ushers inspire supernatural giving by reinforcing everything the Holy Spirit has performed in the service.

Your preparedness affects the outcome of the offerings. If your unpreparedness forces and causes the pastor to fill time by ad-libbing, you are giving Satan an opportunity to remind the congregation of other ways they could spend their money.

Ushers who aren't prepared when it's time for the offering are like a covey of quail. If you have done any hunting, you know that when you come upon a covey of quail (about ten or fifteen quail bunched together) and you walk into them, they take off in all directions. Some ushers don't know where the envelopes are; they don't know where the buckets are; and they just take off in all directions. They run around the sanctuary trying to find the envelopes. They run out in the foyer saying, "Where are the buckets? I didn't know he was going to take an offering now! We always take an offering at the end of service. What is he doing taking one at the beginning of the service?"

So they're running around, and now the pastor has to ad-lib. He has to start making up something, because he sees the ushers are not prepared. While he's ad-libbing, people start to think, "Remember the water bill? Remember that new pair of shoes I saw? They won't be on sale forever."

Unprepared ushers give people time to remind themselves of all the other things they wanted to spend their money on. But we all want to operate in faith don't we? Well, faith is *now*.

The Holy Spirit told the pastor, "*Now* is the time for the offering." He wants everybody in faith—*now*. So he gets up and says, "It's time for the offering—*now!*" The ushers should be up—*now!* The ushers should have the envelopes—*now!* The ushers should have the buckets—*now!* They pass out the envelopes—*now!* The people fill out the envelopes and the checks—*now!* The buckets go by—*now!* They drop their offering in the bucket—*now!*

The buckets go about four people down the row and the people say, "What did I do? I just paid my tithe! This is the first time I ever did it!" Why? Because they did it right then, *now!* Faith is *now!* And they sit there and say, "The windows of heaven are going to open up, going to pour out a blessing on me, which I cannot contain, according to Malachi 3:10. And Luke 6:38 says give and it will be given back to me. I can claim these promises *now*, because I did it!"

Why? Because you, the usher, did it *now!* It was done in faith. People start getting blessed. Why? Because you are helping to serve them in faith—*now!*

One final note—ushers must tithe and give offerings in their personal life before helping to gather offerings. Otherwise they are being hypocritical and not setting a proper example.

Acting, or pretending to believe in tithing if you don't, will eventually show.

Women Ushers

I am often asked, "Can women be ushers?" We are all unique in the body of Christ. We all have a place and a purpose. Yes, a woman can function in the usher's ministry. There are many situations in ushering where a man's presence can create a negative reaction. For instance, in dealing with a woman trying to comfort a crying baby in the service, you would have to agree that a woman usher would be more sensitive and understanding than a male usher. I have seen at times that a wall goes up when a man usher tries to approach a woman in a situation like this. Also, during times of prayer ministry at the altar, the woman usher can assist women and children in a far greater way than any male usher.

Haven't you heard that when God created man, He was in a hurry and as a result, we still have a few rough edges. But when He created woman, He took His time and did it right!

When a husband and wife serve together in an usher's ministry, it portrays to the congregation and to visitors that they are a part of a family church.

I am a firm believer there should be a distinction between men and women when it comes to physical matters. Let me give you an example. During offering time, I would have the ladies handing out the envelopes, the men would be passing the buckets. During communion (what a great time to display the family unit), I would have the ladies passing the bread and the men passing the juice. I believe within the usher's ministry, if there is coffee or any preparation for the guest speakers, this would be a great opportunity for the ladies to minister.

Finally, in Romans chapter 16, Paul asks the church to recognize those ladies who minister faithfully in the body of Christ. What a wonderful scriptural example for the church today.

Usher's Checklist

1. Do I represent Jesus and His Church to the public to the degree

that others enjoy and remember my relationship with them?

2. Do I represent Jesus to unsaved people with my God-like manner?

3. Everyone is special to God, so do I strive to make everyone feel special?

4. Is my sole desire in seating people to preserve order?

5. Do I seat people safely and reverently?

6. Am I accommodating when seating people by trying to meet their requests, or do I provoke them and cause them to avoid me?

7. Are visitors treated with tender loving care and a follow-up greeting after the service?

8. Do I receive offerings with reverence and cheerfulness, and keep the confidentiality involved in counting offerings?

9. Am I invisible when I am assigned to take attendance, or do I like to stir up attention with my presence?

10. Do I try to flow with and accommodate my pastor during altar calls and ministry times?

2
Lifestyle Ushering

Leadership by Example

I am a firm believer that God places spiritual qualifications and priorities first. Ushering techniques only work after your heart is made right before God. You must set a visible, realistic standard of servant-hood in the Church of Jesus Christ. Because your ministry is highly visible, you hold a greater responsibility to serve without any appearance of evil before saint or sinner. A supernatural usher is motivated by a servant's heart and is honored to be a servant to the Lord, the pastor, and to the members of the Church.

Your example of humility, love, diligence, faithfulness and pure-heartedness will bring praise to the Lord, honor to the Church, and the power to minister to needs at every level.

I have seen ushers operate supernaturally while greeting visitors before a service. Sensing a need by the Holy Spirit, they asked people if they needed prayer and subsequently brought about miraculous healings, salvation and deliverance in the lobby even before the church service started.

I have observed Spirit-sensitive ushers seat a couple with marriage problems next to a happily married couple, to help mend their marriage. One of my ushers told how he just sensed in his spirit that this husband and wife were having problems. So he purposed to seat them behind a real lovey-dovey couple in the church, who were always nibbling on each other's ears.

He put them behind that couple so they could see that it is possible to have a good marriage. It *is* possible that you can love one another and have a good marriage. That is what is exciting. In the Spirit-realm you learn these things.

I knew an usher who stopped a man from searching through a pastor's desk after God spoke to him. You must expect God to use you in your capacity as an usher. Your ministry is just as important as anyone else's. This usher was patrolling our parking lot because we were in a part of town where, if we didn't patrol the parking lot, your car might not be there— or *parts* of your car might not be there when you got back. He was out in the parking lot, and he had a good attitude. He was praying over cars that needed prayer, and tires that needed tread.

He wasn't out there complaining, "I don't know why they stick me out here all the time. I wish I could be in there listening to the service. But oh no, we have to be out here. If these people locked their cars, we wouldn't have to stay out here. Look at that one over there, it's unlocked. I'm not going to lock it—it's their fault."

You can have an attitude like that, but don't expect God to speak to you.

This usher was out there serving the people. He was out there praying for the service. He was out there praying over the cars and praying over the tires— praying for families that needed a new set of tires. As he started praying for them and interceding for them, God spoke to him. He heard those words in his spirit by the Holy Spirit.

"There's somebody in the pastor's office going through his desk right now."

He walked in, walked down the hall and saw that the pastor's office door was cracked open about two or three inches. He walked up to the door, opened it up and saw a man going through the drawers in the pastor's desk. He asked him, "What are you doing?" The man said, "I'm looking for the bathroom." The usher said, "Well, the bathroom's not in here."

What did the ushers do with that man? They brought him out and seated him in the sanctuary so that he could hear the Word of God. It was just his word against the usher's word. He said he was looking for the bathroom. But at that moment in time, the ushers were in control.

What was the best thing they could do? Put him in there where the Word of

God was being taught. Let the conviction of the Holy Spirit get all over him. Oh, it's exciting to be an usher. It's more than just passing buckets. That young usher who learned to listen to the voice of God today is the president of Harrison House, the publisher of this book. Luke 16:10 tells us he who is faithful over the least will be faithful over much.

The lifestyle of an usher is outlined in First Timothy and Titus where the qualifications of deacons are defined. Since you are operating as a deacon, you should live by biblical standards.

You may feel I'm overemphasizing the importance of your role. No! Church is a life and death situation. You never know:

- What type of need a person has,

- What life-threatening illness a person is battling,

- What homes are being destroyed, or

- What husbands and wives are contemplating divorce.

People's souls are on the line, so don't pretend to play church if you don't have the genuine needs of people in mind. Didn't Jesus consider Himself a servant of the father? That means that those in the ministry are servants regardless of the level of authority in which they serve.

You can only minister supernaturally by renewing your mind to God's Word and submitting yourself daily to the cross of Jesus Christ. So how do you prepare for such an awesome responsibility?

Part 1: Spiritual Preparation

The first key to effectiveness is spiritual preparation in the form of prayer. Hopefully, the usher team will spend time in unified prayer before the service, so Satan won't gain a foothold during the service.

Prayer is the foundation of all anointed actions and deeds in the Church. It will bring you in tune with God's heart and thoughts, and remove the roadblocks that Satan tries to set up in your church. Prayer also prepares men's hearts to receive God's saving Word.

Pray before you usher in the church so you can tackle your task with spiritual strength and power. Only prayer will bring this. Also, by making praise and worship a vital part of your prayer time, an anointing will come upon your life. Never put your call to serve as an usher above your spiritual relationship and time with God. If you try to appear spiritual or servant-like without prayer, your hypocrisy will find you out.

First Corinthians 13:1-13 sets forth the standards you should live and serve by. Liberally season all you do and speak with love. Your commitment to pray for the unlovable in your congregation will bring the answer of how to reach them.

One man wouldn't shake my hand or acknowledge my presence on Sunday mornings. God gave me the creative idea to greet him cheerfully by name. He progressed over the weeks from taking my outstretched hand, to shaking my hand, to actually giving me a brotherly hug. Most importantly, he came to the point where he could receive love from another member of the Body of Christ.

Cultivate the Five "T's"

Also, cultivate the five "T" qualities: teachability, thoughtfulness, tactfulness, timeliness and teamwork.

Teachability

The teachable usher is willing to learn demanding functions and responsibilities over years of dedication, training and practice.

Thoughtfulness

The thoughtful usher develops a good memory for names. By using concentration, association (connecting a name with a person you know or object that sparks your memory) and by practicing, you will grow in your ability to make people feel special by remembering names.

Tactfulness

Tactfulness is your ability to do and say the right thing without offending a person, especially in awkward situations. You must be able to respond while keeping your flesh under control.

Timeliness

Timeliness is knowing when, how and what to do in every situation. Cultivate your level of alertness and ability to take initiative. Trust your intuition, or human spirit, which should be sensitive to the Holy Spirit's prompting. Listen to your spirit and flow with it, being ready for change when it comes. Also learn timing from seasoned ushers and, above all, learn from your past mistakes.

We had a head usher that I trained under who could smell a wrong spirit when it came into the church. I never saw anything like it. I remember one time we were walking around the church and he said, "There's one in the building." And I thought, "Where is it?" I was a new usher and I didn't know what he was talking about. He said, "We have trouble in the building."

He picked that up in the spirit, because he was responsible for order in our church. So we were walking around, and I was following him really close. He was just checking things, and he stopped, and said, "See that guy right there? There's your problem. Put an usher with him." We brought in an usher and sat him down behind this man.

How did that head usher know the man was going to do something? One thing he did know, if the man did try to cause a disturbance, that usher was right there. If you're not sensitive, people can slip in like this and just stand up and start doing whatever they want to do.

I remember one time when there was a person who slipped into one of our services, one of the ushers picked up something in his spirit about him. He said, "Something's not right about this person. I've never seen him here before, but I know something's just not right. I have a real check in my spirit."

He sat behind this person, and halfway through the service, this person stood up, pulled out a piece of paper and started reading something. Right in the middle of the message, he just stood up. As soon as the man stood up, the usher put his hand on the shoulder of that man and sat him right down. The problem was taken care of just that fast.

Everyone was calm and secure because they knew the ushers were taking care of the situation. I've heard people remark, "You can go to that church down there and hear the Word of God being taught without distraction. The ushers at that church serve you."

I've heard people make remarks like that about ushers and about churches. I don't know about you, but I want to go to a church where I can hear the Word of God.

Teamwork

Ushers work better as a team. Even Jesus knew this when He told the disciples to seat five thousand men and their families before miraculously feeding them with five loaves and two fishes. (Luke 9:14.) Jesus knew that twelve men could seat a crowd more efficiently than one. It is very important that you have regular meetings together. You should discuss how you can better yourselves in serving the people. Make this a time of recruiting new ushers. It is hard to serve as a team if you never meet the other team members and understand each other's responsibilities. A spirit of excellence is what Jesus expects from us.

Usher's Checklist

1. Am I willing to learn and lead with a servant's heart?

2. Am I willing to be an example to God's flock:

   - Even when people don't sit where I want them to?

   - Even when people are unfriendly and unloving?

3. Am I willing to develop a helpful attitude and go the "second mile" with people?

4. Am I dedicated to the task of ushering?

5. Will I allow faithfulness and dedication to take precedence over my talents or outward qualifications?

6. Can I keep a positive attitude? (Can I be an inspiration and not an inflammation?)

7. Can I set a tone of calm reassurance in emergencies and move into action with composure?

8. Am I willing to let God shape, mold and prepare me to be a better usher, or do I always feel like I can do the job better than others and refuse instruction?

9. Do I have the resolve to serve my pastor even when it is inconvenient and difficult?

Part 2: Natural Preparation

Your manners, physical appearance and personal hygiene are crucial as an usher. Don't cause others to avoid you because of correctable situations.

Manners

Never embarrass another person. Learn to be sensitive to people's needs and limits so you can build lasting relationships. Also guard against favoritism. The poorest church member deserves the same warm greeting as the richest member.

Use direct eye contact and a firm handshake (not limp or crushing) initiated by you. Such actions signify warm heartfelt greetings and make people feel like royalty. Don't be too familiar with people, especially with the opposite sex. Some people do not like hugs, so let the people set the boundaries.

Hair

Always keep your hair clean, neat and free from dandruff. Also meticulously trim your beard and mustache before services.

Clothing

Pay careful attention to the condition of your suit or clothing. Clothes actually reflect attitudes like honesty, rebellion, poverty or "I don't care" attitudes. If your suit is dark, watch for dandruff or loose hair on the shoulders.

If you have handled babies or toddlers, check your clothing for milk or food stains. Make sure your pants, shirt and coat are pressed and your tie is straight.

Breath

Overcome bad breath or coffee breath by brushing your teeth before the service. Keep mints in your pockets at all times.

Due to a strenuous workload, use an effective deodorant or antiperspirant, but don't overwhelm people with fragrant colognes, powders or after-shave lotions. You don't want to be responsible for handing out headaches to people sensitive to fragrances!

Shoes

Cleaned and polished shoes are a must. If you don't have an appropriate pair, talk to your head usher. He might be able to make or arrange for the needed investment.

Sickness

If you're feeling feverish or coughing, ask for prayer from the pastor and elders. Do not serve as an usher if you are not healed instantly. Protecting and honoring others means you will not purposely expose them to any type of health problems.

Usher's Checklist

1. Sensitivity

   • Am I sensitive to each individual's limitations and allow them to set the boundaries when I greet them?

   • Do I insist on hugging people regardless of their preferences?

- Do I extend my hand first in friendly greeting or do I wait for others to respond to me first?

2. Greeting the opposite sex.

   - Do I guard my reputation as a usher when I greet the opposite sex?

   - Do both my hands and eyes signify purity and respect for others?

3. Attitude toward the unlovable

   - Do I take the time to be warm and caring toward the unlovable?

   - Do I heed Jesus' command that sick people (weak and needy)need a physician, thus allowing my church to be a refuge for the infirm, hungry and wounded?

- Do I tend to prefer the well-established, upper-class individuals and shun those individuals who don't fit into my standards of acceptability?

3
Down to Basics

Pre-service Preparation

Punctuality

Try to arrive thirty to forty-five minutes before the service to prepare yourself. Also, check to be sure if everything is in order in the sanctuary.

Assignment

Report to the usher in charge and learn your duty assignment. If you are not familiar with your area, refresh yourself by glancing through manuals and walking through the area. Know which aisle you are expected to walk down during your assignment. Know the location of the nursery, telephone and Sunday school classrooms. Also read the church bulletin for the latest information.

A person may come up to you after the service and say, "What were they talking about, about singles doing what? I'm a single." The usher should not say, "Well, I don't know—read your bulletin. I'm not a single. I've been married for years, even though I would like to be single."

Such an attitude tells the person question that even though you're a worker you're really not very interested in what goes on in your church. So why should they be interested? Ushers, read your bulletins. Make sure you have an understanding of what's going on.

Pocket Supplies

Always keep extra pens, pencils, breath mints or hard candy in your coat pocket to loan or distribute to those in need. Anticipate the needs before they arise.

Church Supplies

Check for the proper location of offering plates or buckets, offering envelopes, visitors' cards and other applicable forms that are passed out during a service. Mid-week service ushers can often perform re-supply duties.

Mid-service Duties

Preventing distractions during a service may be one of your greatest challenges. People are easily distracted and often the unsaved are looking for any excuse to escape the wooing of God's Spirit. The enemy often uses innocent children and unruly, disobedient or noisy adults to distract the lost and grieve the Holy Spirit. Disturbances create unhappy listeners who are unable to receive anything from God.

Distractions amount to double-mindedness. James 1:7,8 says a double-minded man is unstable in all ways and will receive nothing from God. Your job as an usher is to eliminate distractions so people do receive from God. Christians should not have to leave a service with their spiritual cup half-full.

If a person causing distractions is not seated at the end of a pew, use an index card to relay a message instead of trying to whisper. Don't allow disturbances to get out of hand before you address them.

Children

Learn how to present the availability of all nursery and children's activities that coincide with regular services. Try to meet incoming parents before they enter the sanctuary. Encourage parents to take their babies to the nursery, especially if the pastor doesn't want children or babies in the sanctuary. If the parent insists on keeping the child (which is often neccessary with a newborn), seat them in the back of the sanctuary and explain how important it is that they exit if the baby makes noise or becomes restless.

Vagrants

Alcoholics, panhandlers and various types of street people will drift into your church, expecting to reap benefits of Christian charity—usually on their terms. Whenever possible, take them to a private place without involving the pastor and assign two seasoned soul-winners to them.

Hallway/Restroom Roamers

Always have an usher assigned to these two areas. Use spiritual discernment and common sense. If adults refuse to cooperate, ask them to leave the church building before you call the police. Often, the troubled person will allow you pray for them. Handle children by escorting them to their parents or an assigned Sunday school classroom.

Distraught Individuals

Mentally distraught or demonically controlled people are often characterized by rhythmic rocking, rolling eyes, irrational movements and constant mumbling or talking themselves. Whether dealing with mental or spiritual problems, such people are extremely unstable and should be handled immediately. Contact the head usher and agree in prayer immediately for God's power to manifest itself. Then ask the person to leave. If the person refuses, ask the head usher to notify the platform.

Your pastor must make the decision whether he wants to handle the problem from the pulpit or have the usher team bodily carry out the person. Such removal can be done so smoothly that only the people near a disturbance need to know.

For example, one pastor noticed demonic activity during a Sunday service and paused during his sermon to ask the congregation to stand for a time of greeting and fellowship. When the congregation stood, the ushers removed the problem person to a counseling room so quickly that no one was aware of the situation.

Elderly

Offer your arm to assist elderly people to their seat. If they prefer to walk on their own, walk slowly to the accessible seat you've chosen for them. Don't show any impatience or irritation. If they take your arm, tell them how far you are going as you walk slowly. Ask them if they have any special needs or might need assistance to the restroom. Above all, always treat the elderly with respect.

At my home church, Church on the Move, Tulsa, Oklahoma, we have valet parking for our senior citizens. We park their cars for them. We have a special room for them, a reception room where they can come in and have coffee and donuts. Pastor Willie George told the senior citizens that we were not doing this because they felt sorry for them, but out of respect for the elders and to honor them. The valet parking became so popular that senior citizens lined up for blocks, especially on a day with bad weather.

When the program first started, there was one gentleman who insisted, "There's no way you're going to park my car, young man. You'll have to carry me on a stretcher before I'll let you park my car." Then it was raining one Sunday and he was the first one there with his car, wanting the church to park it.

The word got around town. "They have valet parking over at that church for senior citizens. You just pull up, and they take your car."

Next, the church went down to a quick lube place and obtained the forms used to check oil, water and tires. Then on Sunday, when the people came for valet parking, the ministry parked the car, then went through the service checklist for the whole car. When the people came out of service, they told them what they had found.

"You're a little low on transmission fluid. You've got a tire that's a little low on air that you need to get checked. You need to get your oil checked—you might want to change it."

One Sunday the church cleaned all their windows. Teenage boys were helping. When the people pulled up, the kids just jumped in and cleaned all their windows and the inside of the car. The church did that for their senior citizens, to honor them. I think that's a great idea. Church should be a great place—an enjoyable place. We're here to serve and to minister to people.

Handicapped

Ask the handicapped person if they need assistance to their seat. Never try to grab the arm of a person on a cane or walker since they may be concentrating on keeping their balance. Also, be aware that stroke victims may lack feeling on one side or may have hearing, visual or communication impairments.

If the person is in a wheelchair, introduce yourself and ask him or her if they need assistance. Don't be over-eager in your attempt to help. Assure them you have sufficient space by the end of a pew and give them a preference as to how close they want to be wheeled near the front of the sanctuary.

Always be aware of the person's comfort and safety when transporting an individual in a wheelchair. Know the mechanics of a wheelchair—adjustable footrests, restraining straps, how to lock and unlock brakes and how to move it safely. Make sure the person's arms are resting inside of the armrests (not hanging down) and secure the feet. Avoid jolting or jerking steps that would throw a person forward. Stay alert!

Never give a handicapped person the impression that he or she is burdensome, frightful or that you are unable to accommodate them. Disabilities are not contagious diseases.

Talk directly to the disabled individual. Try not to focus completely on the person's disability, yet don't ignore it as if it doesn't exist. Sensitivity and common sense instead of pity will help you establish a relationship. If the person doesn't need assistance, then just offer your encouraging presence.

Also tell the person to please signal you or another usher during the service if a special need arises. And try to make provision by the side or rear of the wheelchair for the person's assistant or relative.

Be Sensitive

I once heard of an usher who said to people arriving in wheelchairs, "Wheelchairs on the left!" Some of the guests wanted to turn around and say, "Lady I'm not a wheelchair, I'm a person." We need to realize that *people* are sitting in those wheelchairs. Most people who use crutches and wheelchairs have some kind of pain and are hurting. If they're not hurting physically, they're usually hurting emotionally. Jesus is in you and the most important thing is to extend the love of Jesus.

You are a minister and have in you the same Holy Spirit that raised Jesus from the dead. I look for the day we will see the headline in the newspaper, "Man with muscular dystrophy healed by an usher's prayer."

Ushers Are the First Ones to Talk to People

When people come in on crutches they usually don't talk to anybody. The usher is often the first person they talk to. You represent the church, and you have the opportunity to extend love and grace to those in wheelchairs.

It is important to be sensitive and careful in the way you approach and talk to people, especially those in wheelchairs. Some in wheelchairs cannot get out and would be offended if you asked them to. Others, however, can get out of the chair and sit in a regular chair next to their spouse. Let the person in the wheelchair indicate if they prefer to stay in the chair or sit in a regular seat with friends or family.

Your job as an usher is to accommodate the people coming to the meeting as much as possible. There may be times you have to tell someone they can't sit in a certain place, but do it in a way that will not cause anger and strife. Many times ushers deny requests for their own convenience and not because of church policy or orders from the pastor. Remember, Jesus came to minister to others, and not to be ministered to. As ushers, you are called to do all that is possible to assist those you are serving.

Use the Correct Words

"Handicapped" is a generally accepted word. We use the term *handicapped parking*. There are some people who don't like that word—they don't want to even be thought of as handicapped. But I personally don't know of another word.

Do not use the term *invalid.* Handicapped people are not invalids. There are many people who are physically whole, and they are invalids.

The word *assistance* is better than *help,* and ushers should make an effort to be aware of that. You are here to serve the people—*all* the people. Some people would be insulted if you suggested they need help, but most would be happy to be offered assistance.

Some of the people are going to come in half mad anyway, and they don't like being in a wheelchair. They are half mad at the world and they will take it out on the ushers. Some people think the church owes them. In such cases you have to be patient, just like with anyone else.

Many in wheelchairs will want to sit in their wheelchairs on the floor in the front, and ushers should realize that option is available. The reason they might prefer sitting down front is that for thirty minutes when the service starts, everyone is standing up praising the Lord and those in wheelchairs cannot see. We should have special consideration for those persons who are in wheelchairs, because they can't stand up and they can't see what's going on when everyone else is standing up.

The Handicapped in Prayer Lines

Handicapped persons should be assisted into the prayer line in the same way any other person is assisted. Ushers sometimes are concerned they are hindering the faith of one in a wheel-chair coming to the prayer line.

The person in a wheelchair should be allowed to come on their own, and directed or assisted to the place in the line, to keep everything orderly and allow the minister to get to them. It is an individual judgment call as to how much assistance to give in a prayer line.

Usher's Checklist

1. Am I conscious of the needs of different individuals and do I try to meet them at the point of their need?

2. Is punctuality and dependability a top priority in my ushering commitment?

3. Do I have the ability to deal tactfully, kindly and swiftly when distractions occur?

4. Do I have an efficient system worked out between other ushers for removing problem people?

5. Am I sensitive to the needs of the elderly and the handicapped?

6. Do I try to educate myself with information that will help me specialize my service to them?

4
Special Duties

Seating

God is a God of order. Order will be reflected in the church when His servants are well-trained and listen to His voice. Don't the miraculous feedings of the crowds illustrate His desire for order during His supernatural provision of human need?

It is your responsibility to help people safely and reverently enter and exit the sanctuary. Don't permit your church to have people who fight for seats. One 600-member church was known for the uproar that followed as worshipers entered the Sunday school area at the same time through the same doors that other worshipers were exiting. The free-for-all actually drove people from the fellowship because the searching souls were hurt and dismayed over the display.

Your mission is clear: *Preserve godly order and protect the weak, needy and infirm. Be sensitive, but don't be intimidated.*

Develop a seating system between ushers. For example, when the head usher (who is standing at the entry way to the sanctuary) sees a party of four enter, he catches the eye of the lead usher in the center aisle and holds up four fingers. The lead usher in turn will find four seats. After locating the seats, the lead usher will nod yes, and the head usher will then release the people to go to the lead usher.

The lead usher then greets the party quietly as he leads them to their seats.

Practical Seating Tips

- Your assignment should be centered around a certain area of the sanctuary.

- If seating people before service, ask them for their seating preference. After the service begins, don't ask for preferences. Seat them where it doesn't cause disturbances.

- Reserve the back seats for early departures, latecomers and special-need people. Don't outrun the people you are seating—walk only a few steps ahead.

- If your party stays with you, place your hand on the row or pew in front of the one you've selected and face them. Then the guest knows which row to enter.

- Watch for vacant seats as you walk back the aisles. Know your area so you don't escort people toward the front only to find the seats filled.

Don't reprimand people who slip by you. Stay positive.

- Your responsibility doesn't end after seating takes place. Be alert for discomfort or physical distress among elderly people under a doctor's care.

- During the seating process, try to fill up the front section first while keeping the back section roped off. It is proper to always escort the ladies, but don't disturb a service or embarrass a person being seated by forcing them to sit in the front after the service starts.

- Don't seat people during prayer time or if the gifts of the Spirit are in operation. It is irreverent.

- Don't get so personally involved during the service that you are distracted from your responsibilities. You are to maintain surveillance.

Visitor's Welcome

Although each church has its own method, most churches greet and welcome visitors with a visitor's packet. Be prepared with these so when guests raise their hands, you can offer them the appropriate materials. Carry extra pens and pencils for filling out visitor's cards.

After the service, seek out the visitors in your section and personally greet them. Thank them for their attendance and invite them to the next service. And try to remember their name after meeting them!

Offerings

Techniques for receiving offerings are as varied as church buildings, but most churches station ushers at the front of the church and work toward the back. Larger churches station additional ushers along the aisles. Pass the collection plate to one side of the aisle while receiving the plate from the other side, then reverse the pattern at the next row.

Communion

Since communion was specifically given to the Church by Jesus, it is important the believer's attention is devoted to Christ and not the ushers. Always serve with dignity and revere the presence of the Lord. The congregation will often copy your behavior.

Double the servers since you must distribute both bread and wine. The wives of married ushers make excellent backup ushers. They also display the importance of a family church. Backups do the same work as the regular ushers during communion. You also may need to assign an aisle supplier. This person ensures that the trays of bread and wine are continuously filled. A tray should be considered empty when there are not enough cups or elements to serve a complete row. The aisle supplier should be summoned when a tray is dropped or spilled. Never serve a spilled tray.

Many churches begin communion with the ushers lined up before the podium. They face the pastor while he prays over the two elements. Other churches leave the elements in the back of the sanctuary and have the ushers walk to the front to serve after corporate prayer. Follow your pastor's preference.

Always serve the bread before the juice. Didn't Jesus give the disciples bread first? Some churches assign one set of ushers to serve the bread and another set to serve the juice. I suggest using the women to serve the bread and using the men to serve the juice. Always serve the individuals in the podium area as well as audio/video workers and musicians. You should stand at your assigned position until everyone receives the elements. Then you may sit down unless you have to gather glass communion cups. Glass communion cups can be gathered efficiently by passing empty trays down each row while having the aisle supplier pick up the full trays.

Emergencies

Clear emergency procedures and quick action can make the difference between life and death. Your church should establish guidelines for medical emergencies, power failures, fire evacuation and severe weather. Prominently display emergency phone numbers by every telephone.

- Always assign one person to call 911.

- Station one or more persons outside the building to direct paramedics to the patient's location.

- Keep one usher with the afflicted person at all times. Pray for the person's recovery in faith, and don't allow a crowd to cluster around the person.

- Assign one person to stay with the family or friends.

- Don't leave your usher station, unless called upon by the head usher.

- Help any person in the midst of a medical emergency (heart attack, stroke, seizure, onset of childbirth, exhaustion, fainting or any peculiar symptom) to a private room. Talk to the person about how they feel and what they think the problem is. Relay their answers to health care professionals by telephone or when they arrive. Immediately dial 911 if you have access to this emergency medical response system. Otherwise call the operator. Follow these simple guidelines in order to prevent any trauma or complications.

Heart Attacks

If the person complains of a squeezing chest pain, indigestion, arm pain, nausea, sweating, weakness, lightheadedness or a feeling of "impending doom," have the person sit or lie down. Loosen any restrictive clothing and administer oxygen if available. Calmly reassure the patient. If the person's heart stops, administer CPR (cardiopulmonary resuscitation). I advise all ushers to take this invaluable Red Cross course offered in every community. This simple procedure saves thousands of lives per year.

Seizures

Seizures are caused by high fever, infections, brain injury, stroke, epilepsy and, in rare cases, by demonic oppression. Call for professional help immediately, but take measures to keep the person from hurting himself during convulsions. Don't be alarmed, and at all cost, keep the person's airway clear until they gain full consciousness.

Gently lay the person on the floor on his side in case he vomits or salivates. Loosen restrictive clothing around the neck and chest and place a padded bite stick or piece of leather between the person's teeth only if there seems to be a danger of the individual biting his tongue. Don't use force—you might break teeth or be bitten. Convulsions usually last 1-5 minutes. Hold the arms and legs tight enough to prevent injury, but don't try to hold the person completely still. Some movement allows muscles to move. The person might be drowsy or confused afterwards and won't remember what happened.

Bleeding

Always apply pressure directly over the wound with a clean cloth or your hand. Try to raise the injured part above the level of the heart whenever possible.

Breathing Difficulties

Open the victim's airway and tilt the head back. If an adult stops breathing, pinch the nostrils and cover the mouth with your own. Begin with four rapid breaths and then use one breath every three seconds. If an infant stops breathing, cover both the nose and mouth with your mouth. Use four quick breaths and one breath every three seconds.

Broken Bones

Never move the victim because you must immobilize (keep still) the broken bone. Apply a splint carefully only if help will be delayed, but don't attempt to reset the bone.

Burns

Relieve the pain of minor burns with cold water and protect from contamination.

Serious burns need medical help but in the interim apply large sterile dressings to protect the area from contamination. Also treat for shock.

Heat Exhaustion

Hot summer days and cold winter days may cause people to feel unusually weak or faint. If they are faint, don't administer food or drink. Have them sit or lie down and apply cool compresses to the back of the neck and forehead until medical personnel arrive.

Childbirth

Assist a woman with labor pains to a private place. Encourage her husband to stay with her and reassure and calm her. Call her doctor immediately and summon an ambulance if the woman desires. Don't try to delay or restrain the delivery. Remember that nearly every baby before 1900 was born at home or in places less sanitary than your church building. Relaxation is the most important key to a healthy, natural delivery in situations like this.

Diabetics

Diabetics must control their blood sugar levels through insulin and normal food intake. Insulin without a normal meal may make their blood sugar too low. Then they need candy or a sugar-based substance. If they fail to take their insulin, they may suffer from seizures, nausea or other serious side effects. Call medical care professionals immediately.

Attendance

Establish a non-distracting attendance tallying system you are comfortable with and stick to it. Don't use outrageous antics like telling jokes or distracting movements like slapping a friend on the back while taking attendance. Be invisible. If possible, take your count from the back or from a high vantage point unseen by the people.

Overflow

You should have a plan for an overflow. What would happen if Sunday morning,

3,000 people showed up in a church that seats 1,500! Some ushers would say, "Well, I wouldn't know why they'd want to show up." And that's probably why they don't. I don't know about you, but I want as many people that want to be a part of the service to come.

But what are we going to do with them? Some may say, "Well, this is great, we'll just pile them in here, man, I mean elbow to elbow." No, you need to have a plan on what you're going to do with overflow people. "Oh, we'll just put them everywhere—we'll put them up in the bleachers over here and put them all the way up here and we'll hang them off the balcony up there." You had better hope the Fire Marshal doesn't show up either.

The head usher should have a seating plan for overflow crowds approved by and complying with the regulations of the local fire department. Know the plan by heart. Set up folding chairs in the aisles, balcony or foyer according to the plan. Keep track of vacant seats all the time. Let the head usher or a designated usher handle the traffic flow.

Immediately after the service, remove the folding chairs and carefully turn in any lost purses, jewelry or Bibles in your church's lost and found department.

Altar Calls/Prayer Room

Be your pastor's extra eyes and ears during every altar call. People accepting

Christ may be shy and timid after raising their hand to make a commitment, and your pastor may not be able to spot them because of bright spotlights or bad visibility. Always try to remember the people who raised their hand.

If the pastor doesn't see them, discreetly raise your hand to catch the pastor's eye and point to the unnoticed converts from the back of the room. If a person doesn't rise when called, you may gently approach him and offer to accompany him, but never force or embarrass people.

Creative Solutions for Your Church's Needs

You are the helping hand of the body of Christ. As you serve the needs of the people, situations can often take an unusual turn. For instance, I built a unique corps of ushers at the large inner city church where I presided as head usher. Many of the ushers were off-duty policemen. When our parking lots became the target of car thieves, our ushers carried handcuffs and routinely stopped and handcuffed the thieves and brought them into services to hear the Gospel.

Another time a robber grabbed the offering money as the usher team was taking it to a counting room. Much to the amazement of the police, one of the ushers chased, tackled and handcuffed the robber.

You may not face these problems, but you may have areas that need creative solutions. Larger churches should invest in police-style walkie-talkies with earphone attachments. These battery-powered units fit under suit coats and allow instant communication over several city blocks.

Always anticipate needs. Store extra umbrellas on rainy days and keep a sturdy pair of jumper cables available on cold winter days. If you are in an area that gets snow and ice you should store the necessary equipment to get people out of snow and mud. If the usher team cannot take care of a problem, arrange for the person's transportation—never leave a person stranded at the church.

Finally, never lose sight of the fact that your task as an usher is just as important as the role of those in leadership. God's rewards for your work will be based on your degree of faithfulness. God cannot force you to be faithful to His will and plan for your life. You must decide to be faithful and trustworthy. Proverbs 28:20 promises that the faithful servant will abound with blessing.

When you set your heart to watch after other people's welfare, God will take care of your needs and welfare in ways you never imagined. Always be one of those loving people who serve. God is looking for living sacrifices.

Usher's Checklist

1. What "mission" should I keep in mind when seating people?

2. What technique is most often used
    for ushers when receiving offerings?

3. Do I understand emergency proce-
    dures?

4. What does Proverbs 28:20 promise
    the faithful servant?

Duties of Parking Lot and Security Personnel

PURPOSE: To extend the love of God
through the church by serving in God's
excellence by assisting to park vehicles
in a fashion in order to maximize the
facilities available, maintain order, and
ensure safety to all people attending

services as an extension of the Helps Ministry and the Pastor.

- Come prepared to minister in love to the people attending the worship service.

- Workers are to arrive 40 minutes before each service.

- Be properly dressed in appropriate attire with your name tag. Make sure your appearance is excellent including:

    A. Shoes that are shined

    B. Fingernails that are clean

    C. Breath that is in order and pleasant

D. Hair that is neat and clean

Parking Area

- Be at your assigned location 30 minutes prior to all regular services or as directed by your team leader.

- While working as a team, park the vehicles in an orderly fashion, each row and each space to be filled in order to maximize the total facility to its fullest.

- If time permits, shake the people's hands, assist them getting out of the vehicles, shelter them with umbrellas (if the weather dictates), and most of all, give a warm and sincere smile and greeting. This is your Father's house—make them feel they are special and desired at His house.

- Some workers may be assigned to help the elderly, seniors or pastors with assistance from their cars to the building. You will be briefed on any special items and procedures.

- Cars should be parked in a fashion to allow safety of all personnel. This usually means parking vehicles in the same direction, filling the closest spaces first and in order.

- Team leaders should release as many personnel as possible to attend services, keeping only enough personnel to handle the necessary latecomers. Keep in mind, late arrivals know they are late and probably had a tough time getting to church. Encourage them, tell them they will be blessed and that something special is awaiting them.

- Use all available space, allowing as many women to stay off the gravel lot and on the pavement as possible, due to high heels and stability of the ground.

- Park buses and oversized vehicles out of the way. Have them unload near the door and park them out of the main parking traffic patterns.

5
Usher's Proverbs

1. You are ordained and anointed by God and divinely set in the church for a purpose.

2. An usher's job is just as important as highly visible leaders in the church.

3. Biblical ushers are like the deacons described in the New Testament. You are to be a trustworthy man who

handles the duties of ruling and serving God's people.

4. Ushers should strive for the reputation of men like Stephen, full of faith and the Holy Ghost. (Acts 6:3-5.)

5. Ushering duties encompass four specific areas: assist the pastor, meet and greet people, maintain order and receive offerings.

6. Ushers represent Jesus and His Church to the public. You delight in making people feel special.

7. God places spiritual qualifications before ushering techniques. Keeping your heart right before God makes you a visible, realistic standard of servanthood in the local church.

8. A supernatural usher is a servant to the Lord, the pastor and church members.

9. An usher sensitive to God's Spirit expects God to use him and meet the needs of people through prayer and action.

10. Ushers must view church as a life-and-death situation whereby souls are on the brink of life-changing decisions.

11. An usher spiritually prepares himself through personal prayer and corporate prayer with other ushers. You understand that prayer is the foundation of all anointed action and deeds in the Church.

12. The ideal usher liberally seasons all he does and says with love. You make an effort to love the unlovable.

13. Ushers utilize the five "T's"—teachability (willing to learn), thoughtfulness (remembers names), tactfulness (speaks right things without offending), timeliness (knows what to do and when to act) and teamwork (able to work with others).

14. Ushers cultivate good manners, a pleasing and neat physical appearance and excellent personal hygiene.

15. Ushers never embarrass other people, show favoritism or insist on actions (like hugging) that might irritate others.

16. Ushering involves preventing distractions that would hinder people from receiving God's Word.

17. Ushers learn to handle all types of people with compassion and wisdom —children, vagrants, church roamers, mentally ill, elderly and handicapped.

18. An usher's responsibility includes helping people enter and exit the sanctuary and be seated properly in a safe and reverent manner.

19. A good ushering team develops a workable seating system for the beginning and middle of church services.

20. The ushering team understands and always improves the flow of specific

events like offerings, communion and water baptism.

21. A prepared usher knows the medical recourse for all emergencies.

22. An usher is a pastor's eyes and ears during altar calls and special times of ministry.

23. Ushers are creative problem-solvers when it involves the special needs of the church.

24. God rewards ushers according to their degree of faithfulness.

25. When an usher sets his heart to watch out for the welfare of others, God takes care of his every need.

PART 2

Legal Do's and Don'ts

The Legal Do's and Don'ts for Ushers!

The first and foremost *legal* concern an usher will face is the issue of what type of actions will, or could potentially lead to, criminal sanctions. The most commonly used phrase you hear is an "assault and battery."

Assault and battery is, by *legal* definition, an unlawful or non-permissive touching. In fact, an *assault* is the threat and subsequent realization by a victim that they are about to be struck. The *battery* is actually the second part of the action and is the unlawful touching, which is technically a second and distinct crime. These definitions and accompanying advice must be prefaced by the fact that every state and local community has its own separate, distinct body of laws governing criminal behavior. Therefore, you should always check with a local lawyer, or your church's attorney, for specific laws which govern your particular state and locality.

Use Verbal Control When Possible

If a member, guest or anyone else attending your church becomes unruly or loud, you might be faced with a decision of how to remove the troublesome person from the service. Your first course of action should always be a polite, discreet request that the individual please step out of the service until the problem is resolved. If the individual refuses or becomes belligerent, you will now be faced with a choice—physically remove them or let them continue to disrupt the service!

You should now be mindful of the fact that your status as a church usher *does not* give you permission or authority to drag the person out of church by their arm. If you do so, you have committed an unpermissive touching which is unlawful, and would constitute a battery upon that person.

This fact holds true regardless of whether the person is a church member or a first time guest. Your course of conduct should be to insist upon the person leaving the service so that orderly worship may continue.

Be careful to remember this when dealing with children. They are afforded the same protection under the law as adults. You may not grab up several little rowdy boys and stick them in a back pew with instructions to keep quiet! Nothing prohibits you from giving those little bundles of energy a minor scolding with *verbal instructions* to settle down while staying quiet in a back pew. Employing godly wisdom and good usher training will adequately prepare you for these inevitable encounters.

There may be occasions where force or physical "touches" will be allowable. Please keep in mind that you should always seek a peaceful solution which does not lead to physical contact. As an usher, there may be the rare occasion when you are needed to break up a fight, remove a guest who is physically threatening others or a similar type event. In most states, you may counter force being used against you with equal force. For example, if someone raises his fist towards you, unequal force would be revealing a baseball bat with spikes! In any event, if you are ever faced with a physical threat which is likely to place you in grave physical danger, or is deadly, you may always counter with equal measure.

The most difficult problem for an usher is also the most likely scenario—a member or guest of your service is faced with danger from an angry spouse or irate visitor. Most criminal statutes do not allow you to use force to protect a third person. Your most appropriate action is to try and dissolve the dispute, If this fails, try and separate the two parties. Using physical force against the aggressor can potentially lead to criminal problems for you! Again, your use of physical force should be extremely rare and, in this particular situation, used only to separate two sparring individuals.

Confidentiality

Another issue ushers face deals with a different concept—confidentiality requirements. An usher is not generally thought of as a pastor or minister with whom religious, confidential discussions are held. Moreover, you do not need to exercise this right of confidentiality if you choose not to do so. An example or two should bring this to light.

A member comes up to you after a service and tells you that they feel as if the pastor was out of line with his message, or that perhaps a staff member was rude to the member. You are not *legally charged* with keeping this information confidential. You may share the discussion with the pastor, your usher captain or even your wife. Of course, always use godly discernment when discussing such a matter with others, particularly if it is of a "gossipy" nature.

Furthermore, you may encounter a situation where a member shares suicidal or criminal actions with you in a confessional manner. You are not legally bound to remain quiet about this information, and may freely approach your pastor or usher captain about possible actions and/or prayer to undertake.

Regardless of the situation, an usher is involved in the ministry of helps with their church, and this should be your attitude and approach to every responsibility you undergo. While there are legal concerns ranging from an unlawful touching to confidentiality requirements, they will almost certainly be far and few in your service if you are using servant qualities similar to our Lord Jesus Christ!

PART 3

The Head Usher

The Head Usher

As a head usher, you have a high and holy calling! Your example and leadership as an usher is what will inspire others to serve. Your work actually corresponds closely to the duties of the early deacons appointed in the first century. The following Scripture is useful as a model to help you train ushers at every level of spiritual maturity:

In like manner the deacons [must be] worthy of respect, not shifty and double talkers but sincere in what they say, not given to much wine, not greedy for base gain [craving wealth and resorting to ignoble and dishonest methods of getting it].

They must possess the mystic secret of faith [Christian truth as hidden from ungodly men] with a clear conscience. And let them also be tried and investigated and proved first; then,[if they turn out to be] above reproach, let them serve [as deacons].

[The] women likewise must be worthy of respect and serious, not gossipers, but temperate and

selfcontrolled, [thoroughly] trustworthy in all things.

Let deacons be the husbands
of but one wife, and let them
manage [their] children and their
households well.

For those who perform well
as deacons acquire a good standing for themselves and also gain
much confidence and freedom
and boldness in the faith which is
[founded on and centers] in
Christ Jesus.

1 Timothy 3:8-13 AMP

1
Responsibilities of The Head Usher

Decision Making

Because the functions and responsibilities are demanding, not every person can do the work of an usher. It takes years of dedication, training and practice to master all the aspects. As the administrator over this department, you need to develop the ability to make quality decisions and be on the alert for the type of individuals who would make faithful entry-level workers. Simply accepting everyone who wants to be an usher is as dangerous as accepting a person who can't sing into the choir.

I guide my decisions in placing people in the ministry of helps with this motto: *be leery of those who seek authority but grab hold of those who want responsibility.*

Some people only want authority. If a person offers to usher, let him read the guidelines you've compiled for ushers. Then if he is still interested, require the person to read this book. I believe a person should be willing to follow your specific guidelines and then bear fruit in the position of an usher.

Ask God to give you the ability to lead others by example and with a servant's heart. You want to cultivate ushers who can blend love with firmness and not be weak-willed pushovers. Training them to do everything in love even when they aren't treated or respected properly will develop men strong in Christ.

Appreciation

Never neglect the area of people appreciation. Always thank your workers for their faithfulness and commitment to show up on time and handle their responsibilities in a professional way. Try to devise ways to express your gratefulness. For example:

- Appreciation letters acknowledging the person's invaluable contribution to the ministry

- A yearly appreciation banquet or luncheon

- Quarterly newsletter featuring ushers' contributions

- Birthday recognition activities (even sending a birthday card)

- Summer picnics

- A holiday party

Be sincerely creative in devising your system of appreciation. Your gratitude for a "job well done" will encourage your staff to always put 100 percent commitment and loyalty into their job.

Communication

You must always maintain open communication with the ushers under your care. They must feel they can approach you with their problems or concerns and not be criticized. Knowledge eliminates fear because fear comes with the unknown. Giving your people knowledge will eliminate the questions of "what if...."

Keep written guidelines updated and distributed to your ushers. People cannot serve properly without knowing the rules and regulations of the job. The more lax you are in establishing guidelines, the more situations will grow out of control. Let each person know their responsibilities in accordance with your church policy, and never grow impatient with the training process. I remember being involved in a church that took two years to train workers.

Always distribute monthly ushering schedules (which include each individual's area of responsibility) in advance so each usher has an opportunity to submit any necessary changes to you. Be flexible enough to make concessions if an occasional commitment prevents an usher from serving on his appointed day. Remember—God did not appoint you to be a dictator, but to follow Christ's example as a shepherd.

Also, distribute an updated list of the names, addresses and phone numbers of the ushering team. This allows the ushers to contact another usher as a substitute (unless you set up a different system of notification for cancellations).

Overwork

Don't overwork your ushers by utilizing the faithful ones for every service. Try to develop a rotation system so if an usher has to work one service he is able to sit with his family and hear God's Word during the second service.

I recommend an usher serve a one-year term of service with the option to renew his commitment. You never want an usher to overcommit to the detriment or neglect of his family. Be creative in your scheduling. If a certain individual is extremely busy but wants to usher, perhaps you can use him for out-of-the-ordinary meetings, or as a last-minute substitute for someone who might cancel.

Budgeting

Your organizational skills have an impact on how efficiently your department runs. Work out an appropriate budget with the finance department that allows you to purchase the necessities used in your department. For example, if you hand out mints or cough drops to church members in need, don't expect each usher to purchase these with his own money. Don't make ushers bring their own umbrellas to assist people from the parking lot on rainy days. Keep a well stocked supply area.

Always keep inventory of your supplies like offering envelopes, pencils and other needed items. If necessary, develop a system that allows you to submit a requisition order to the church office (or whoever orders supplies) at least two weeks in advance. Don't be caught envelope-less in a big service!

Have an area within the church that is the usher's station. Keep it neat and organized so each usher knows where to locate things. You also might want to post a copy of my "usher's prayer" enclosed within this book. This will keep each usher's eyes on his goal of rendering help and assistance to the body of Christ.

Offerings

Most importantly, develop a water-tight system of removing offerings from the sanctuary and counting the money. Don't allow your workers to set down buckets for one second, thus tempting someone to steal the money. Always maintain accountability by having a minimum of two counters in a room at one time. And keep tight security around this area, especially if your church gathers large offerings.

2
Preparing for Guest Speakers

Usually when a pastor invites a speaker, it is to help motivate, train, edify and impart wisdom to the members of the church concerning the Word and will of God in their lives.

There are many preparations and details to handle when a church invites a guest speaker to minister. Many times the ushers' ministry will care for guest speakers.

Arrival Preparations

Before the speaker arrives, make sure that the hotel arrangements are confirmed and that you have personally checked the room. Check in the guests and make billing or payment arrangements with the hotel.

Hotel Checklist

Make sure the room is:

• Clean

• Comfortable

- Spacious

- Smells good

- A king-size bed or 2 queen-size beds

- Air conditioning (on if needed)

- Heat (on if needed)

Guest Information

Leave in Room:

1. List of telephone numbers for the church/pastors

2. Information on transportation pick-up for services

3. Map of church or building location

4. Schedule of events, dates and times

5. Welcome card

6. Flowers

7. Fruit basket

8. Refreshments: drinks, snacks, mints, etc.

These are things that will help make your guests comfortable and rested from their trip before ministering, and will help them to minister to the needs of your congregation, visitors and guests.

3
Church Security
and Safety

With the increase in crime in our cities, both urban and rural, churches have become vulnerable to the same crime that could happen anywhere else in our communities. Churches are no longer necessarily the place where you can go to find safety and security. We have become too liberal in our thinking and closed minded to the idea that "it won't happen in our church."

Vagrants come in off the streets, seeming to look for salvation, but staying only long enough to get a "hand out" to replenish their liquor or drug supply. They solicit for money, becoming loud and unruly without any regard to those attending service.

People bring their domestic problems from home. Women seeking safety are beat at the church doors and even pulled from church by a deranged spouse. Members have been shot at and wounded, sometimes fatally.

No matter how large or small a church is, there are certain precautions it can take to protect itself. The most important thing is to pray for guidance and protection.

> **Be of sober spirit, be on the *alert*. Your adversary, the devil, prowls about like a roaring lion seeking someone to devour.**
>
> **1 Peter 5:8 NAS**

> **The thief cometh not, but for to steal, and to kill, and to destroy.**
>
> **John 10:10**

With some wisdom, common sense and a watchful eye, many problems we face can be stopped before a service is disrupted or anyone is aware that something has taken place.

While attending camp meeting at a very large church in the midwest, two men began to argue near the back of the sanctuary. One was in his mid to upper fifties, the other was much younger. The elder man punched the younger in the face. Within a matter of seconds ushers removed both men without any disruption to the church service.

Just recently, a six-year-old boy ran across a busy street in front of a church location and was hit by an oncoming car. Within seconds safety and security people were alerted, 911 was called and Christians were praying. Traffic was diverted to another street even before the public safety officers could come and do their duty. The driver of the car was overcome with grief and sorrow. The staff and members got to minister, encourage and reassure the driver that all was going to be fine. They even drove him home. The public safety officers commended the church for their action. The boy and the driver both are doing fine and going to church.

Here are some suggestions that you may want to follow as a Head Usher.

Get in touch with the local law enforcement agencies in your area (sheriffs, public safety, state police, etc.). We have found that they are more than eager to help you in establishing a preventive action plan to help protect the church public. Ask them questions regarding your church's physical location. Have them walk through the entire church meeting location. They can inform you of doors and windows that may be easy to access or storage rooms, hallways and staircases that might be easy places to set traps. Let them watch how the offering is taken and handled to offer suggestions to reduce the risks of problems occurring.

Usually these officers don't charge for any consultation. But if they do, it can be well worth it in the end. It would be best to have the agents on your side before an incident happens instead of being unprepared if you must make a 911 phone call.

Some agencies are for hire—usually at a far more reasonable rate than a security agency. Not only will you have an officer on staff who is fully armed, but an entire law enforcement agency to back him up. He is also prepared in case of a medical emergency and can summon help at a moment's notice.

Train ushers to keep their eyes open to be wary of their surroundings and people coming in and out. Just as shepherds had sheep dogs that could spot the predator before he could attack the sheep, ushers must keep a watchful eye over their flock.

One thing you would want to eliminate is a "lazy or slothful" attitude with the offering. Take up the offering and move it out of the flow of traffic quickly. Don't stand in the middle of the service with the offering, striking up a conversation with others. Get moving! Have one or more individuals watch hallways, corridors, staircases, etc.

If you don't count the money during the regular church service, place the offering in a safe immediately. Also, make sure that more than one individual is involved in the transfer of the offering to its safe location. Reasons are plain. Watch out for each other and watch each other. Many robberies take place without anyone picking a lock.

Some churches make deposit runs from their location to the bank night deposit. This involves radio communication between two vehicles that will leave church simultaneously. The lead car carries the offering, driven by a dedicated officer of the church who has the night deposit key and is accompanied by a security member. The second vehicle follows keeping radio communication with the first vehicle. His responsibility is to watch the flow of traffic and report if any irregular activity is taking place near the bank location.

Selecting Your Security Personnel

These individuals should be people who are dedicated, of good report, committed to the pastor's vision and the vision of the church. You should screen these individuals more carefully than those of other departments. Individuals with a law enforcement background can usually be a plus to your staff. Watch out for hot shots or those who think they are Barney Fife. This is a ministry just like any other in the body of Christ.

Your security staff should be visible, but not to the point that the congregation can dictate their actions. They should know the rules and regulations established by the church administration governing their position. The hired security staff are just that—hired to do a job—not to socialize and fellowship with the congregation. The congregation should be made aware that they are present, but not pointed out or introduced formally.

In smaller churches the security staff is usually consisted of either the deacons and elders or the usher staff. Either way these individuals should be considered trustworthy, loyal, of good report and carry the vision of the church in their heart. Faithfulness and loyalty are very important. Imagine going into battle with another soldier who would not report to duty nor attend boot camp for training. He would come in when he wanted to and not listen to commands. He could not be trusted in the field of battle.

Look for people, men or women, with the qualities that were previously described. In our church, we don't publicly announce that these positions are open—we recruit on a one-on-one basis. I always

ask that potential candidates pray first
and speak to their spouse before making
a commitment.

4
Other Head Usher Tasks

Departmental Meetings

Keep your pastor informed on the time and place of your organizational meetings. Encouraging his attendance and input at your meetings on an occasional basis will be a great morale builder for your workers. You will also know his expectations of your team.

At your meetings, encourage your workers' input. Write down areas of improvement as well as areas of complaint. Keeping a record of your meetings and attained goals will give your group a sense of accomplishment. Try problem solving as a group and listen to each person's concerns.

Encourage the ushers to share success stories of how effective one of the ushering methods has been. An usher may have a testimony on how his persistent love and friendliness toward an introverted person finally brought them around.

I also would send a meeting review sheet to the pastor if he isn't able to attend your meetings. Keep him informed of any changes and gain his approval for new proposed policies. In other words, don't restructure the entire church without his involvement!

Starting Up

If you are just instituting an ushering system, you will need to set up the guidelines and procedures for the following areas:

- Attendance—counting

- Children—dismissing, monitoring

- Communion—supply, distribution

- Emergencies—medical, weather

- Maps—visitor and staff maps with location guides

- Offerings—receiving, counting money

- Praise and Worship

- Sermon Activities—pre-service, interim, post-service

I also recommend that you write down your policy guidelines and distribute them to your ushers. The following sample will give you an idea of how to lay out guidelines for your ushering staff. Please modify them according to the needs of your church structure.

- Absenteeism—Please honor the day and time you are scheduled. If you are unable to usher, please contact the head usher with a twenty-four hour notice, whenever possible, so a substitution can be made.

- Confidentiality—Information and details concerning church members, the church office or people's contributions are private matters never to be discussed.

- Dress Code—Please wear a neatly pressed suit and tie. Sandals and thongs are not acceptable. No heavy colognes.

- Health—Do not usher if you are fighting a cold or communicable disease.

- Incident Reports—Please report in writing if you are hurt on the premises or witness an incident whereby another person is hurt.

- Sign-in—Please sign in and out for an accurate record of volunteer time. This is helpful if you have an awards program.

- Training—Orientation procedures include reading *Ushering 101*, familiarity with church building layout and several weeks working beside an experienced usher.

- Department Change—A person may move to another department or change an assignment to another area of interest after obtaining approval by the head usher.

- Termination—When an usher becomes counter-productive, the head usher arranges a discussion session. If violations continue, dismissal occurs. A open door policy for concerns or ideas is maintained at all times.

Fearlessness

If God is calling you to be the head usher, He will give you the love, ability and fearlessness to do it. Always look at your ministry with a fresh eye. When I worked in the church, I would evaluate my department every three months. I would

look at what I was doing and ask why. I
would also ask myself if God put me in the
position or if I placed myself there.

5
Usher's Prayer

The following prayer was designed for you as you undertake the challenging and rewarding task of ushering.

Father, I thank You that I'm involved in the supernatural ministry of helps. You have placed me in the church to render help and assistance to the weak and needy, to the body of Christ, to my pastor.

Help me to see that all things are done decently and in order. Make me a hedge of protection about Your sheep so they can be fruitful hearers and not distracted double-minded listeners who receive nothing from You.

I ask for wisdom, Lord, to clearly see and know Satan's devices. I know I bodily represent Your kingdom of righteousness and truth. Make me a man of prayer that is sensitive to Your Spirit and able to thwart the devices of the wicked one.

Allow me to view each of Your children as precious and holy because I seek to be an extension of Your hands and heart. Grant me the right words in due season and the ability to serve and meet the needs of others.

Father, I thank You that I am led by Your Spirit and made in Your image and authority. You have given me the power to warn the unruly, comfort the feeble-minded and support the weak. I believe You are cultivating the mind and attitude of Christ within me.

Allow me to maintain the attitude of a joyful servant and give You all the glory. Thank You for allowing Your perfect will to be done in this supernatural ministry of ushering You have committed to me.

In Jesus' name, Amen.

PART 4

Questions and Answers

Questions and Answers

Q. The most difficult part of ushering is seating people who don't want to sit where I ask them. How do I handle this situation?

A. Roping off and opening sections as needed often solves this dilemma. If you have the manpower, use an usher to stand at a row until it is filled. Don't panic over the people who refuse to be escorted. Your only two choices for people who sit in a roped-off section is to ask them to move or leave them alone. Remember, though, you are dealing with all kinds of people with all types of burdens. Therefore you must maintain a kind and peaceable attitude and try to prepare them to receive God's Word. Your job is not to provoke or harass people. Difficult situations often test the fruit of the Spirit within you.

Q. How do I handle problem people who constantly walk out during a service or wander in the hallways?

A. Communication is the key to understanding a situation. Talk to the person privately without embarrassing him. There may be a medical reason the person has to leave during the service. If this is true, reserve a convenient, non-distracting seat for this individual. Also kindly explain to them the distraction it causes when a person moves around during a service.

Q. You mentioned the occurrence of actual physical attacks against ushers or pastors. How do you prevent these incidents?

A. Ushers must move quickly in potentially threatening situations. If a person is acting peculiar in actions and attitudes, follow your instincts and watch them closely. If the Holy Spirit puts a check in your heart about an individual, don't ignore it. Of course, you don't dismiss a person from the church without obvious reason—but seat the individual where you have immediate access to him. If the person starts to move, put a hand on his shoulder and address him immediately. I believe the larger the church, the more Satan will bring in troublemakers to stir up disturbances.

Q. I would like to usher, but I dislike dressing up. Why are clothing guidelines necessary?

A. Each church department needs guidelines in order to maintain order. Because the usher is responsible for greeting visitors including non-Christians, I believe he should set an example. He is the individual who makes the first, and often lasting impression, on others. I believe the dress code example set by the pastor is the highest authority. What the pastor wears before the congregation is what the ushers should wear. He sets the tone.

I also believe a person must make concessions in areas that are not particularly pleasing to him. An effective usher must have a servant-like heart and be willing to conform to the guidelines of the church, even if this involves wearing a suit and tie.

Q. After serving faithfully as an usher on my assigned days, it seems like I am always needed to work additional services when others don't show up. Then I cannot sit with my family or hear God's Word. Am I wrong in starting to resent this?

A. All workers need the opportunity to listen attentively to God's Word during a service. Your works will die if your faith is not built upon the Bible. I never recommend working people until they die spiritually or leave the church. The person in authority over you needs to sensitize himself to your needs. Explain your situation to this person and suggest the possibility of rotating workers.

Q. Why is teamwork among ushers so important?

A. Ushering in an organized way involves a team operation, not a group of individuals following their own paths. You need to set up guidelines for every situation and try practice runs until you get the operation down smoothly. For instance, if every usher is bumping into each other as he tries to seat people, confusion will result and undermine the confidence of the people coming into the sanctuary.

Do not work against each other, and never wait until you have an awkward situation to try to figure out how to handle it. Always know the who, where, what, why and when, especially when you are expecting large numbers of people for a service.

Q. How do I handle another usher who is trying to undermine me and push me out of my position in the church?

A. Pray for God to bring the situation to the attention of the head usher or pastor. Don't retaliate with similar actions. Keep your attitude consistent with the fruit of the Spirit and continue to do your work in the most excellent way possible. God is able to take care of the situation if you try to overlook the shortcomings of others. Always practice self-examination with questions like: Am I where God wants me? Am I maintaining godly attitudes and actions?

Am I doing everything in my power to walk in peace with my brother?

Q. I feel more qualified to lead our usher team than the person presently in charge. Should I talk to the pastor or head usher about assuming more leadership?

A. Elijah, the mighty man of God, sets the perfect example. In First Kings 18:36-37, he declares, **Let it be known this day that thou art God in Israel, and that I am thy servant....** Elijah understood that God does not move on account of one's status, title or natural accomplishments. God moves on behalf of one's faithfulness and service. God will open the door of promotion for you—if that is His will—as you quietly and faithfully serve under another person. God hears the prayer of servanthood.

Q. I am bored with ushering and feel like I am not appreciated in our church. Should I leave and possibly start my own ministry?

A. First, I would pray for God's direction. When God is leading you to do something, He usually reveals enough to guide you in the right direction. But don't move out of boredom. You might be trying to mold and shape yourself. Let God fashion you into what He wants as you serve in the church. It is not always enjoyable when you feel you can find a more exciting position.

But reaffirm your resolve to serve
your pastor until God clearly shows
you where He wants you.

Suggested Reading List

The Ministry of Helps Handbook
Rev. Buddy Bell, Harrison House, 128 pages

This handbook combines both spiritual and practical guidelines for serving in the church. Ideal for motivating a person to faithfully fill a position in the local church.

Management: A Biblical Approach
Myron Rush, Victor Books, 236 pages

This management-oriented book is based on the premise that people are God's most valuable resource. This helpful guide addresses issues like: communicating effectively, nurturing good relationships, managing time, making decisions and solving problems. Recommended for those who lead and manage others.

Your Gift of Administration
Ted. W. Engstrom, Thomas Nelson Publishers, 171 pages

This practical handbook for Christian administrators stresses how to encourage and maintain enthusiasm in others. In addition, it covers the importance of accountability to God, delegating responsibility and the benefits of careful planning.

Life-changing books by John C. Maxwell:

The Winning Attitude,
Thomas Nelson Publishers

Developing the Leader Within You,
Thomas Nelson Publishers

Be a People Person, *Victor Books*

Be All You Can Be, *Victor Books*

Deuteronomy Commentary,
Communicator's Commentary Series, WORD, Inc.

Tough Questions—Honest Answers,
Here's Life Publishers

Think on These Things, *Beacon Hill Press*

Church Growth: Everybody's Business,
E. LeRoy Lawson and Tetsunao Yamamori,
New Life/Standard Publishers, 152 pages

Authors challenge ministers, deacons and elders to make disciples for Christ by understanding the church growth process and the role of the church in a changing world. All phases of church growth are covered from home to abroad.

Leaders
Harold Myra, editor, CTI/Word Book, 208 pages

This twelfth volume in "The Leadership Library" series includes candid interviews with 16 proven Christian leaders. Each person honestly shares the triumphs and trials of leadership. Interviewees include such individuals as U.S. Senator Mark Hatfield, Senate Chaplain Richard Halverson, business executive Fred Smith and J.C. Penney's retired CEO Donald Seibert.

Leadership Explosion: Maximizing Leadership Potential in the Church
Philip King, Hodder & Stoughton, 190 pages

This informative resource book for leaders and potential leaders is based on the premise that healthy church growth is based on programs that develop people's potential. Leadership styles in different cultures, denominations and congregations are also explored.

Spiritual Leadership
J. Oswald Sanders, Moody Press, 255 pages

Encourages men and women of God to place their natural talents and spiritual qualities at God's disposal so He can create great leaders. Sanders uses biographies of men like Moses to illustrate the principles of spiritual and temporal leadership.

Spiritual Leadership, Responsible Management: A Guide for Leaders of the Church
Michael T. Dibbert, Zondervan, 207 pages

This practical handbook is based on the premise that the church needs spiritual leaders with management abilities. The author effectively unites New Testament models for leadership with good management principles. All types of spiritual leaders—elders, deacons and board members—are addressed.

Church Alive
Peter Cotterell, Inter-Varsity Press, 127 pages

Cotterell utilizes his experiences as an Ethiopian missionary for 20 years to share church growth principles for ordinary churches. He offers searching questions as well as advice for Christians seeking new levels of productivity within the church.

Quick Reference Index

Rev. Buddy Bell, president and founder of the Ministry of Helps International, Inc., in Tulsa, Oklahoma, originally began serving in the ministry of helps in his local church by doing with excellence all his hand could find to do.

Sensitive to the leading of the Holy Spirit, Rev. Bell began developing highly effective methods of ushering, conspicuous only in their reflection of God's character and love. Ushers following his example or trained by him functioned supernaturally. As they maintained the order necessary to allow the power of the Holy Spirit to flow forth to minister, they spread God's love. People's needs were met not only in the services, but elsewhere in the church building, even in the parking lot. Consequently, churches began requesting Rev. Bell's usher and general ministry of helps training.

Rev. Bell began holding workshops, speaking at conferences, serving as a consultant to churches, filming videos and writing manuals and books to meet the need. His training, coupled with his hilarious presentation, have been in great demand. He has now traveled to more than 1,000 churches, teaching and helping church staffs and congregations awake to the power and plan of the Holy Spirit for accomplishing the work of the ministry through every believer.

Rev. Bell has authored *The Ministry of Helps Handbook* revealing how to be totally effective serving in the ministry of helps. He has also produced "The Complete Local Church Usher Training System," "Development of Local Church Leadership Notebook" and 20 videos utilized by more than 5,000 churches worldwide.

Rev. Bell's humor, zeal and anointing from God to present ministry of helps training motivates people in a most delightful manner to find their place and fulfill their ministry in the local church.

Videos and Other Books by Rev. Buddy Bell
Videos (VHS Only)

The Local Church - Leadership Series

Faithfulness: The Crowbar of God

God Uses Both Stars & Candles

Jesus and the Ministry of Helps

Fear Not: Leadership, Organization, Structure

Guidelines: Yes or No?

How to Motivate Volunteers

Straight Talk to Leadership

The Local Church - Motivational Series

The Zeal of God

The Word Works

How to Close the Door on Strife and Jealousy
in the Local Church

Staying on Track with God

How to Deal with Burnout

Journey of a Servant

The Local Church - Helps Series

Understanding the Ministry of Helps

Finding Your Place in the Local Church

How to Relate to Your Pastor

Winning First Time Visitors

The Local Church- Servant Series

Ushering in the Local Church

The First Look - Host & Hostess

Why Minister to Children

Manuals

The Complete Local Church Usher Training System

— The most complete course for ushers available

— Two-hour video and 70 page training manual

Development of Local Church Leadership

— Bring organization and efficiency to the local church

— Eight cassette lessons and study notes on leadership

Book

The Ministry of Helps Handbook

To contact the author, write:

Ministry of Helps International

P. O. Box 27366

Tulsa, OK 74149

(918) 245-5768/FAX (918) 245-2466

Additional copies of this book are
available from your local bookstore

Harrison House
Tulsa, OK 74153

Prayer of Salvation

A born-again, committed relationship with God is the key to the victorious life. Jesus, the Son of God laid down His life and rose again so that we could spend eternity with Him in heaven and experience His absolute best on earth. The Bible says, **"For God so loved the world, that he gave his only begotten Son, that whosoever believeth in him should not perish, but have everlasting life"** (John 3:16).

It is the will of God that everyone receive eternal salvation. The way to receive this salvation is to call upon the name of Jesus and confess Him as your Lord. The Bible says, **"That if thou shalt confess with thy mouth the Lord Jesus, and shalt believe in thine heart that God hath raised him from the dead, thou shalt be saved. For whosoever shall call upon the name of the Lord shall be saved"** (Romans 10:9-10,13).

Jesus has given salvation, healing and countless benefits to all who call upon His name. These benefits can be yours if you receive Him into your heart by praying this prayer:

Heavenly Father, I come to You admitting that I am a sinner. Right now, I choose to turn away from sin, and I ask You to cleanse me of all unrighteousness. I believe that Your Son, Jesus died on the cross to take away my sins. I also believe that He rose again from the dead so that I might be justified and made righteous through faith in Him. I call upon the name of Jesus Christ to be the Savior and Lord of my life. Jesus, I choose to follow You, and ask that You fill me with the power of the Holy Spirit. I declare that right now, I am a born-again child of God. I am free from sin, and full of the righteousness of God. I am saved in Jesus' name, Amen.

If you have prayed this prayer to receive Jesus Christ as your Savior, or if this book has changed your life, we would like to hear from you. Please write us at:

Harrison House Publishers
P.O. Box 35035 • Tulsa, Oklahoma 74153

You can also visit us on the web at
www.harrisonhouse.com

The Harrison House Vision

Proclaiming the truth and the power

Of the Gospel of Jesus Christ

With excellence;

Challenging Christians to

Live victoriously,

Grow spiritually,

Know God intimately.